# A Tune a Day
## For 'CELLO

## A Second Book
### for Violoncello Instruction
### in Group, Public School Classes
### or Individual Lessons

[ *Provides training in ensemble playing when*
*used with the Violin and Viola books* ]

*By*

## C. PAUL HERFURTH

## BOOK TWO—INTERMEDIATE
## TEACHER'S MANUAL
*A complete guide for teaching "A TUNE A DAY"*
*for either Violin, Viola or 'Cello;*
*containing piano accompaniments*
*A very convenient book for home practice*

### THE BOSTON MUSIC COMPANY

DISTRIBUTED BY

HAL•LEONARD®
CORPORATION
7777 W. BLUEMOUND RD. P.O. BOX 13819 MILWAUKEE, WI 53213

B. M. Co. 9589

# DICTIONARY OF TERMS AND SIGNS USED IN MUSIC

For volume of tone:

*pp* —Pianissimo, very soft.
*p* —Piano, softly.
*mp*—Mezzo-piano, rather softly.
*mf*—Mezzo-forte, rather loudly.
*f* —Forte, loudly.
*ff* —Fortissimo, very loud.
*sf* —Sforzando, strong accent.   (> ᴧ)
*cresc.*—Crescendo, gradually louder.  (◁═══)
*dim.*—Diminuendo, gradually softer.  (═══▷)

For tempo (speed):

Largo—Very slow.
Adagio—Slow.
Andante—Rather slow.
Andantino—A little slower than Andante.
Moderato—Moderately fast.
Allegretto—Lively, but not too fast.
Allegro—Fast.
Vivace—Faster than Allegro.
Presto—Very fast.

For increasing tempo:

Accelerando (Accel.)—Gradually faster.
Stringendo (String)—Suddenly faster.
Più mosso—A steady, faster speed.

For decreasing tempo:

Rallentando (Rall.)—Gradually slower.
Ritardando (Rit.)—Gradually slower.
Meno mosso—A steady, slower speed.

For style:

Animato—With spirit, with animation.
Agitato—Agitated.
Allargando—Broader.
Cantabile—In a singing style.
Dolce—Sweetly, softly.
Espressivo—With expression.
Legato—Smoothly, connected.
Maestoso—Majestically.
Con Spirito—With spirit.
Staccato—Detached, separated. (ᵛ)
Tenuto—Sustained. (−)
A Tempo—In the original time.

Other signs:

D. C. Da Capo—From the beginning.
Fine (fee-nay)—Ending.
D. S.  Dal Segno—Go back to the sign (𝄋)
Hold (fermata)—Prolongs the time of a note or rest. (𝄐)

# TO THE STUDENT

**To all the 'cello pupils who use this book:**

This is a personal letter to you. I want you to read it and carry out carefully what I have asked you to do, and during the year let me know, through your teacher, how you are progressing.

Having completed the study of Book I, you should be thoroughly familiar with the fundamentals of good 'cello playing, such as a good position, correct use of the fingers through the proper position of the left hand, and the elementary principles of bow control.

Book II includes a continuation of the elementary material, presenting slightly more advanced exercises and pieces, introducing the 3rd, 4th and 5th positions.

To be better able to play the familiar melodies and pieces, it is recommended that you carefully prepare the purely technical exercises at the beginning of each lesson where a new key and finger-placing is introduced.

Study carefully the diagrams introducing new keys and fingerings so as to properly place your fingers for the new notes. Remember, that you must first read the note and then place the finger, so be sure to know exactly what note you are reading and the proper finger-position for that note. The surest way to play well is to be able to read well.

To be able to think quickly, the following points regarding each note will make you a better player and will make your path to good 'cello playing easier:

      (1) **Name of note** (natural, sharp or flat).
      (2) **How to play** (finger-position and string).
      (3) **How long to hold** (time-value).

I could go on telling you about each lesson, but I must leave this to your teacher. If you do what he tells you, you will go through the pages of this book to the joys and pleasures of making your 'cello sing beautiful melodies.

Wishing you all the success your work deserves, I am,
Yours for good 'cello playing,

*C. Paul Herfurth.*

P. S.—Many of my pupils from each school have formed groups which meet at the different homes to play the duets, trios, and quartets with piano, thus forming a little orchestra. Why don't you try it, you will have lots of fun?

# TO THE TEACHER

In compiling Book II, I have tried to carry out in slightly more advanced material the fundamental principles of good 'cello playing as set forth in Book I.

The material and grading has been carefully done, so that each new step is a logical one for the progress of the pupil. Adequate preparation for the development of the student has been provided for, although the amount of purely technical material has been kept to a minimum. The contents of this book is very largely made up of folk-songs and other familiar melodies of good musical quality, arranged in duet, trio, and quartet form, through which the pupil will be acquiring the fundamentals of bowing and finger (intonation) technic, as well as a consciousness for good musical design and harmonic structure.

The use of the piano accompaniment (Teacher's Manual) should prove of value both in the classroom and in the home. That important advantages will result from its use is certain. The interest and ambition of the pupil will naturally be stimulated through the addition of the harmonic structure which will also serve as a guide to the proper placement of the fingers through hearing the tone he is producing in the harmony. The use of the piano part is recommended from the earliest stages so as to stimulate the musical ear to a nice perception of modulations and harmonies, for which the 'cello, as regards these matters, is comparatively imperfect.

Class teaching should be a combination of individual instruction and ensemble playing. At every lesson there should be individual playing so that all the necessary corrections can be made. Never allow pupils' mistakes to go unnoticed, since only in constant correction will they develop the habit of careful thinking and playing.

A decided advantage of group-teaching is that it provides experience in ensemble playing and gives every pupil the opportunity of listening to the others, of observing their mistakes, and of hearing the corrections.

For the best results each class ought not to number more than six for a half-hour lesson and twelve for an hour lesson. Irrespective of the numbers, the teacher must see to it that there is individual instruction as well as general directions to the class.

Classes should be regraded whenever necessary so as not to retard the progress of the brighter students, nor to discourage the slower ones. Regrading also acts as an incentive for greater effort on the part of the pupils.

It is recommended that every student practice at least forty-five minutes a day. This course provides one lesson a week for a school year.

The eventual success of each pupil depends on regular and careful home practice, according to directions. If possible it would be well for the teacher personally to keep in touch with the parents.

C. PAUL HERFURTH.

# PUPIL'S PRACTICE RECORD

| | SEPT. | | | | | OCT. | | | | | NOV. | | | | | DEC. | | | | | JAN. | | | | |
|---|---|---|---|---|---|---|---|---|---|---|---|---|---|---|---|---|---|---|---|---|---|---|---|---|---|
| | 1 | 2 | 3 | 4 | 5 | 1 | 2 | 3 | 4 | 5 | 1 | 2 | 3 | 4 | 5 | 1 | 2 | 3 | 4 | 5 | 1 | 2 | 3 | 4 | 5 |
| Monday | | | | | | | | | | | | | | | | | | | | | | | | | |
| Tuesday | | | | | | | | | | | | | | | | | | | | | | | | | |
| Wednesday | | | | | | | | | | | | | | | | | | | | | | | | | |
| Thursday | | | | | | | | | | | | | | | | | | | | | | | | | |
| Friday | | | | | | | | | | | | | | | | | | | | | | | | | |
| Saturday | | | | | | | | | | | | | | | | | | | | | | | | | |

| | FEB. | | | | | MAR. | | | | | APR. | | | | | MAY | | | | | JUNE | | | | |
|---|---|---|---|---|---|---|---|---|---|---|---|---|---|---|---|---|---|---|---|---|---|---|---|---|---|
| | 1 | 2 | 3 | 4 | 5 | 1 | 2 | 3 | 4 | 5 | 1 | 2 | 3 | 4 | 5 | 1 | 2 | 3 | 4 | 5 | 1 | 2 | 3 | 4 | 5 |
| Monday | | | | | | | | | | | | | | | | | | | | | | | | | |
| Tuesday | | | | | | | | | | | | | | | | | | | | | | | | | |
| Wednesday | | | | | | | | | | | | | | | | | | | | | | | | | |
| Thursday | | | | | | | | | | | | | | | | | | | | | | | | | |
| Friday | | | | | | | | | | | | | | | | | | | | | | | | | |
| Saturday | | | | | | | | | | | | | | | | | | | | | | | | | |

Always Record Practice Time in Minutes. All Practice Time Lost Must Be Made Up.

# WEEKLY GRADE

NAME ............................................ ADDRESS ....................................

TEL. .................... SCHOOL .................... GRADE ....................

| | Sept. | Oct. | Nov. | Dec. | Jan. | Feb. | Mar. | Apr. | May | June | Tests |
|---|---|---|---|---|---|---|---|---|---|---|---|
| 1st Week | | | | | | | | | | | |
| 2nd Week | | | | | | | | | | | |
| 3rd Week | | | | | | | | | | | |
| 4th Week | | | | | | | | | | | |

E—Excellent; G—Good; M—Medium, Distinctly Above Passing; L—Low, Doubtfully Passing; F—Very Poor, Failure.

# LESSON 1
## Review of Keys Studied in Book I

*Exercises No. 4, 5 and 6 cannot be played with violin class, but may be used with violas.

B. M. Co. 9589

Copyright 1940, 1967 by The Boston Music Co.
International Copyright Secured
Printed in U.S.A.

# LESSON 2
## Studies for the Use of the Second Finger
### One new tone, C natural on the A string

The importance of being able to read notes as well as you can read the letters of the alphabet cannot be overestimated. This is the foundation on which your future progress depends. You must also know the exact position of your fingers on the fingerboard so as to be able to play any given note; for example, to play C♯ on the A string, the third finger is placed a whole tone from the first but to play C natural, the second finger is placed one-half tone from the first. Therefore, the necessity of knowing whether the note is natural, sharp or flat is perfectly obvious.

Have a picture of the fingerboard in your mind in order to see where your fingers are placed for the different notes.

Study the following diagram showing position of notes already studied and the new note to be taken in this lesson. Name the whole and half tones.

NEW NOTE

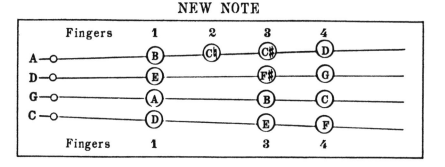

Name the following notes, finger used, and on what string played.

*Exercise No. 3 cannot be played with the violin class, but may be used with violas.

B.M.Co. 9589

# Familiar Melodies Using the Second Finger

## Lightly Row

## The First Noël

Con moto (With motion)

## Home, Sweet Home

Henry R. Bishop
(1786-1855)

Andante (Slowly)

# LESSON 4
# G Major Scale and Arpeggio

*Exercises 1 and 2 cannot be played with violins.

## Duet

**Practice both parts**

Pupil

Pupil

## America
### (My Country, 'Tis of Thee)

Attributed to Henry Carey
(1690-1743)

**Andante (Slowly)**

Pupil

Pupil

## Little Study

Franz Wohlfahrt
(1833-1884)

*Whole tone — stretch 2nd finger.

*Home work*: Mark with this sign ∧ the half steps in both parts of exercise No.4. Write 4 times the G Major scale marking the half steps and placing the sharp. Manuscript sheet, page 7.

# Continuation of the key of G
### Exercises in crossing from C natural to F#

## Duet

Hohmann

Practice both parts

## Little Waltz

Hohmann

Tempo Waltz (In waltz time)

*For teacher or advanced student.
*Home work:* Mark half steps on this page the same as before.

B. M. Co. 9589

# LESSON 6

## Flow Gently, Sweet Afton
### (Quartet)

James E. Spilman

Andante (Slowly)

## Evening Song

Moderato (Moderately fast)

Robert Schumann
(1810-1856)

*rit., abbreviation for ritenuto — gradually slackening the speed.

B. M. Co. 9589

# LESSON 7

Two new tones, F natural on the D string and B flat on the G string.  Study the following diagram so as to *visualize* the exact position of these two notes upon the fingerboard.

Practice both parts on the double staff in this and the following lessons.

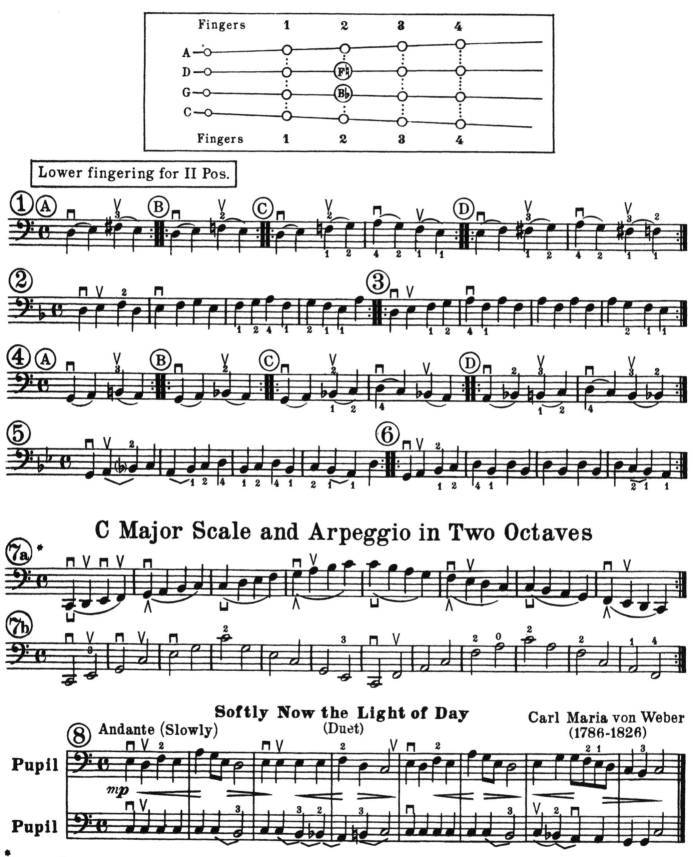

## C Major Scale and Arpeggio in Two Octaves

## Softly Now the Light of Day
(Duet)

Andante (Slowly)

Carl Maria von Weber
(1786-1826)

7a and 7b cannot be played with the violin class.

*Home work:* Write C Major scale 4 times, marking the half steps. Also fill in blanks in above diagram.

B. M. Co. 9589

Learn to take particular notice of the key signature before playing.

## America, the Beautiful
(Duet)

Allegretto (Brightly)

Samuel A. Ward
(1847-1903)

Pupil

Pupil

## Ensemble Part **

** Ensemble parts when used with violins and viola form a string quartet.

## Go Down, Moses

Andante (Slowly)

Negro "Spiritual"

*Stay in the 2nd position while sounding open A.
*Home work*: Mark the half steps on this page.

B. M. Co. 9589

# LESSON 9
## Continuation of the key of C Major

### Russian Hymn
#### (Duet)

Lento (Very slowly)

**Pupil**

**Pupil**

*Stretch 2nd finger.
*Home work:* Mark the half steps on this page as before.

B. M. Co. 9589

## Onward, Christian Soldiers
### (Trio)

Sir Arthur Sullivan
(1842-1900)

B.M.Co. 9589

Note carefully the key signatures and what they mean.
*D.C.* — Da Capo–to beginning.
*Fine* — End

**Melody**
(Trio)

Franz Joseph Haydn
(1732-1809)

① Moderato (Moderately)

Pupil

Pupil

Teacher

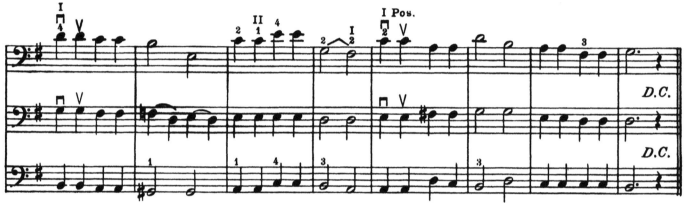

**English Morris Dance**
(Duet)

② Allegretto (Brightly)

Pupil

Pupil

ENSEMBLE PART

③ Andante (Slowly)

**Melody**

Ludwig van Beethoven
(1770-1827)

## LESSON 12
# Christmas Carols

### Hark! The Herald Angels Sing
Felix Mendelssohn-Bartholdy
(1809-1847)

### O Come, All Ye Faithful
Latin Hymn

### Silent Night, Holy Night
Franz Grüber
(1787-1863)

### Silent Night, Holy Night

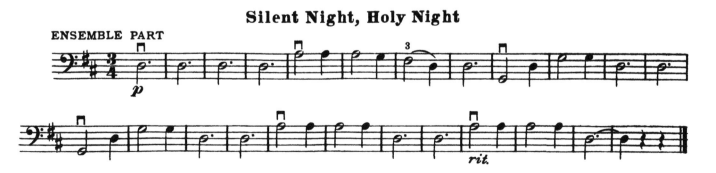

# Review of the 2ⁿᵈ Position on the G and C String

In shifting from one position to another, the thumb remains in the same relative position with the hand, i.e. under the neck of the cello and opposite the second finger.

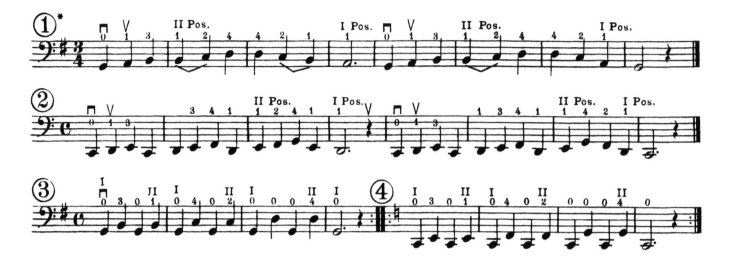

**Little Scale Study**

**Duet**      Henning

*Exercises 1, 2, 3 and 4 cannot be played with violin class.

*Home work*: Mark the half steps as before.

B. M. Co. 9589

## Long, Long Ago
(Scotch Melody)

Thomas H. Bayly

### Duet

Jacques Féréol Mazas
(1782-1849)

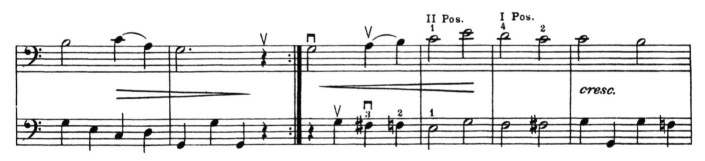

*D.S. *Dal Segno* — Back to the sign (𝄋).
*Home work*: Mark half steps.

## The Little Sandman

Johannes Brahms
(1833-1897)

## Theme from "Military" Symphony

Haydn

## First and Second Ending

The term 1st and 2nd ending applies to one or more measures in brackets at a double bar; thus when the strain is repeated, the first ending is omitted and the second ending played instead.

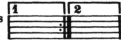

### College Song

B.M.Co.9589

# Key of F Major

Key of F Major, one flat (♭). The flat (♭) placed on the 2nd line of the staff, just after the clef sign, affects every B throughout the piece. Refer to diagram to see the exact position of this note on the fingerboard.

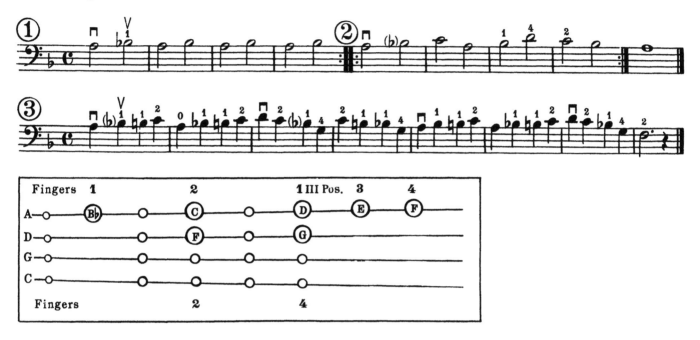

## Scale and Arpeggio of F Major
### Half Steps A to B♭ and E to F

**Con moto**

**Deck the Hall**

Old Welsh

*Home work:* Write F Major scale 4 times, mark the half steps.

B. M. Co. 9589

## LESSON 17
# Continuation of the key of F Major

### All Through the Night

Old Welsh Song

### Santa Lucia

Neapolitan Boat Song

### Little Study in F

\* Andantino — Slower than Andante.
\*\*See diagram in Lesson 7 for position of this note.

B. M. Co. 9589

# Six-eight time

Count six beats to each measure in slow tempo— an eighth note (♪) being the unit of a beat.
Count two beats to each measure in fast tempo— a dotted quarter note (♩·) being the unit of a beat.

Preparatory exercise. Repeat each of the following measures until the rhythm of the different groupings is memorized. Play on the open strings. *Count aloud.*

Notice key signature and finger accordingly.

Play exercises slowly at first, gradually increasing the speed.

Play the D Major scale different ways using the various rhythm patterns indicated above.

The above tune may be used as a round by dividing the class into two or four groups.

**G Major Scale**

*Home work:* Write 4 lines of notes, using different groupings in $\frac{6}{8}$ time dividing into measures.

R. M. Co. 9589

# LESSON 19
# Detached Notes of Different Values in One Row

*Bowing drill:* Practice this line carefully, gradually increasing the speed.

## Oats and Beans

Old English

Allegretto (Brightly)

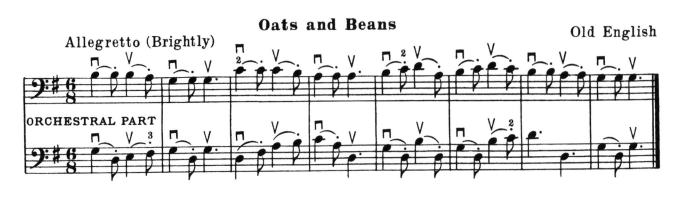

ORCHESTRAL PART

## Mulberry Bush

English Folk Song

Allegretto

## See Saw, Margery Daw

Nursery Rhyme

Allegretto

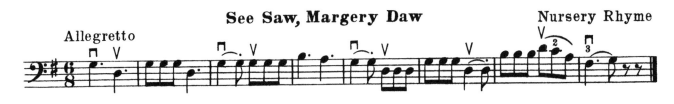

## Hey, Diddle, Diddle

Nursery Rhyme

Allegretto

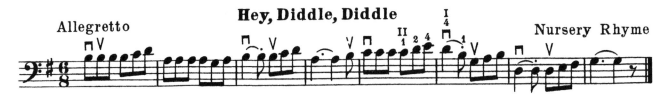

## Old English Morris Dance

Allegretto

\* Use lower fingering for 2nd position.

B.M Co. 9589

# Continuation of 6/8 time

## Drink To Me Only With Thine Eyes

Old English Air

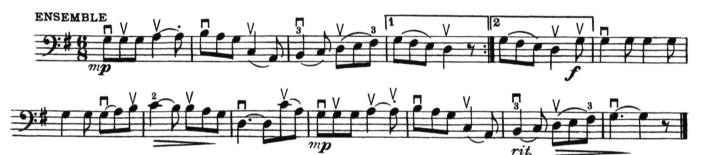

## It Came Upon a Midnight Clear

Richard S. Willis
(1819-1900)

## Scale Study

B.M.Co. 9589

Note: All manuscript pages are to be used for home-work according to instructions

B.M. Co. 9589

# Key of Bb Major

Key of Bb. Bb and Eb. See diagram for position of Eb on the D string. Review position of Bb on the G string in Lesson 7.

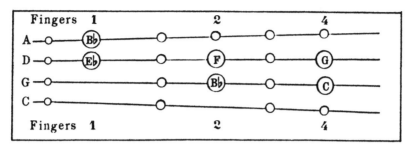

# Scale of Bb

Half steps D to Eb, and A to Bb. Play also in quarter notes.
Review position of Bb on the G string in Lesson 7.

*Home work*: Write the scale of Bb 4 times, marking flats and half steps.

B. M. Co. 9589

### Vesper Hymn
(Trio)

Old Russian

**ENSEMBLE PART**

### A Capital Ship
(Marching Song)

March time

Old English Tune

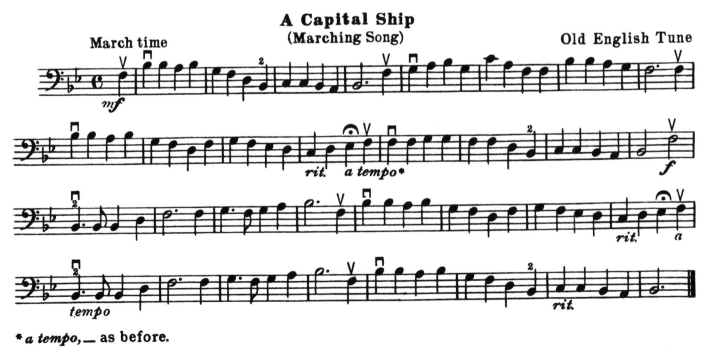

* *a tempo,* — as before.

B.M.Co. 9589

# Continuation of the key of B♭ Major

**Scale Study**

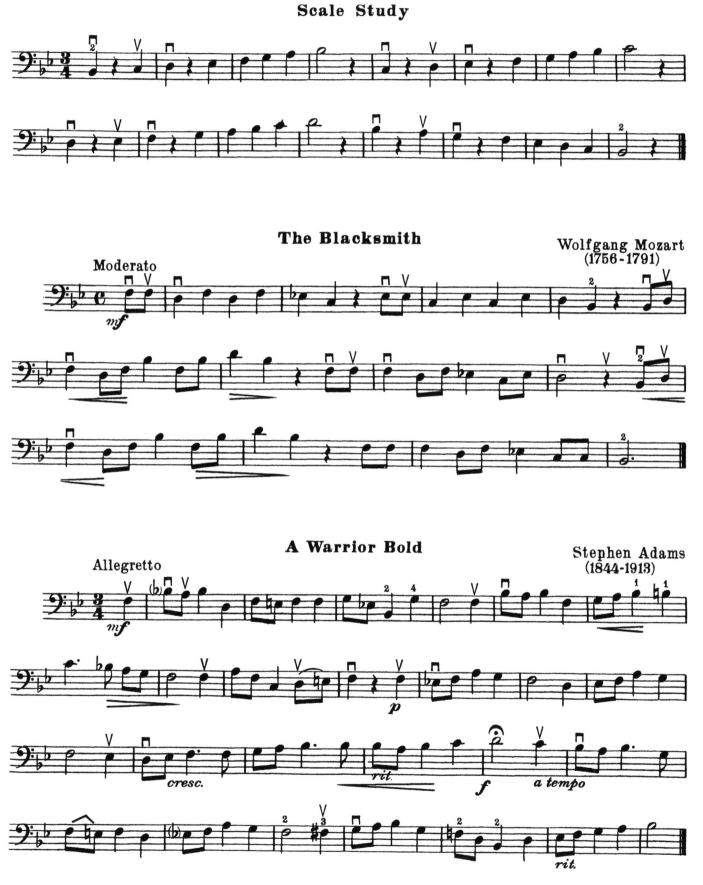

**The Blacksmith**

Wolfgang Mozart
(1756-1791)

**A Warrior Bold**

Stephen Adams
(1844-1913)

# LESSON 24*

## Key of E♭ Major, B♭, E♭ and A♭

### Scale of E♭ Major, upper octave
#### Half steps G to A♭, and D to E♭

### My Old Kentucky Home
Stephen C. Foster
(1826-1864)

*Exercises 1 to 6 cannot be played with violin class.

### The Star-Spangled Banner
John Stafford Smith
(1750-1836)

*Home work*: Write the E♭ Major scale 4 times marking half steps and flats.
Memorize the National Anthem.

B. M. Co. 9589

# Key of E♭ Major—name the flats

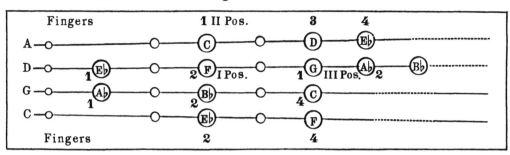

## Scale of E♭ Major in two octaves

Recite the notes of all scales studied.
Use different bowings as in other scales, and play also in quarter notes.

Above scale not to be played with violins.

**Austrian Hymn**

Haydn

*Home work*: Write the E♭ Major scale in two octaves, 4 times marking as before.

B. M. Co. 9589

## LESSON 26
# Key of E Major

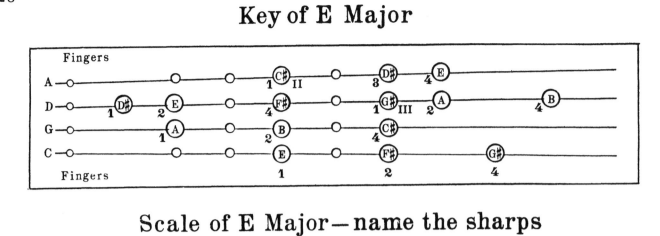

## Scale of E Major—name the sharps

Above scale not to be played with violins.

Place a sharp before the notes affected by the signature in the exercises and pieces on this page.

### Folk Song

### Cradle Song
Brahms

*Home work*: Write the E Major scale 4 times, marking as before

B.M.Co. 9589

# Key of A Major

**PREPARATION**

Place a sharp ♯ before the notes affected by the signature.

**Chimes of Dunkirk**

See diagram above for lower octave of this scale.

## Scale of A Major in two octaves

**O Worship the King**

Haydn

**Pupil**

**Teacher**

\*By very lightly touching the string with the fleshy part of the third finger, we will sound the first harmonic of that string, one octave higher than its open tone. In playing harmonics all other fingers must be lifted.

*Home work*: Write A Major scale in two octaves four times, marking as before, also the fingering used.

# LESSON 28
## Sixteenth Notes

A sixteenth note 🎵 is equal to half the value of an eighth note 🎵 Two sixteenth notes equal one eighth note 🎵 = 🎵 and four sixteenth notes equal one quarter note 🎵 = 🎵

Abbreviations for sixteenth notes 🎵 = 🎵 🎵 = 🎵

### Bird Song
#### Duet

In this piece, which requires a slow movement, it is better to divide the $\frac{2}{4}$ time into $\frac{4}{8}$ (one count to each eighth.)

### Kingdom Comin'

# LESSON 29
# Dotted Eighth and Sixteenth Notes
### Legato (Connected)

This is one of the more difficult rhythms to learn. The dotted eighth note is equal to three sixteenth notes. Always feel a division of four on each beat when playing this rhythm, three on the

dotted eighth and one on the sixteenth

BE SURE TO PLAY THE DOTTED EIGHTH NOTE LONG ENOUGH AND THE SIXTEENTH NOTE SHORT ENOUGH.

### Legato (Connected)

## Largo
### (New World Symphony)
### Trio

Anton Dvořák
(1841-1904)

Use lower fingering for Positions.

B.M.Co. 9589

# LESSON 30
# Dotted Eighth and Sixteenth Notes
## Staccato (Detached)

Dotted eighth and sixteenth notes played staccato (detached) are separated by a short pause, the bow however must NOT be lifted from the string.

These are generally played in one bow with a very crisp stroke of the wrist. Use upper half of bow. During the break between the two notes the bow is held pressed on the string.

## Tramp! Tramp! Tramp!
### (Civil War Song)

George F. Root
1820-1895

## Battle Hymn of the Republic
### (Civil War Song)

William Steffe

B.M.Co. 9589

# Triplets

Triplets are groups of three notes played in the time of two notes of the same value. They are indicated by a figure 𝟑 and a slur placed over or under a group of three notes.

A measure of 2/4 containing two triplets is the same as a measure of 6/8 in march time,

### Pilgrim's Chorus
(Tannhäuser)

Richard Wagner
(1813-1883)

## Alla Breve or 2/2 time

Alla Breve, or cut time ¢ is played the same as 2/4 time. Each note having half the value as in 4/4 time, a half note being the unit of a beat.

### Softly Now the Light of Day

Von Weber

### College Song

## Staccato Bowing

Staccato, meaning detached, separated, is a style of bowing used in violin playing to denote a short crisp note. Notes to be played staccato are marked with a dot, placed over or under them. Draw the bow with a short, quick stroke, and then suddenly stopping it for a short rest, during which the bow is pressed firmly on the string. With this stroke the vibration of the string is stopped, which gives the short staccato effect.

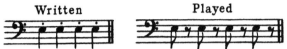

**Andante**
from "Surprise" Symphony

Haydn

## Chromatics

The word "chromatic" means moving by half steps. Chromatic (literally, colored) is well chosen, for by the use of sharps and flats, tone color or shading is added to the natural sounds of the note. A chromatic interval is one half step above or below the given note. A chromatic scale is a scale that ascends or descends by half steps. In playing chromatics the finger must move quickly to the new note so that no slide is heard.

**Etude**

Wohlfahrt

## Pizzicato

Pizz. means to pluck the string. The bow is held against the palm of the hand by the second, third and fourth fingers, the first being free to do the plucking. The tip of the thumb is placed against the corner of the fingerboard under the C string.

**Amaryllis**

Henri Ghys

*Not to be played with violin class.

B. M. Co. 9589

## Sweet and Low
### (Quartet) *

Joseph Barnby
(1838-1896)

*For string quartet, cello play fourth line part.

B. M. Co. 9589